WHISTLING WILLIE

from Amarillo, Texas

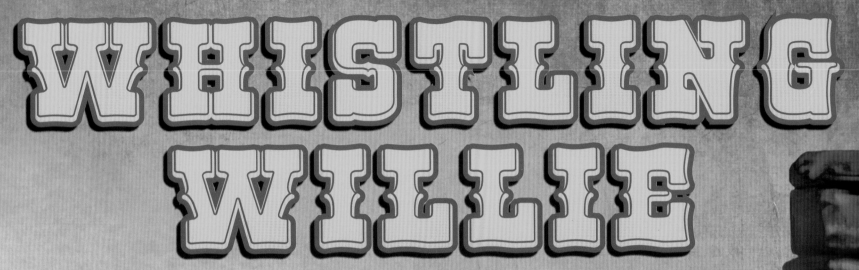

WHISTLING WILLIE

from Amarillo, Texas

Jo Harper and Josephine Harper
Illustrated by David Harrington

PELICAN PUBLISHING COMPANY

GRETNA 2015

To Jamie Julian Harper—J. H. and J. H.
To my wonderful cousins Jackson and Riley—D. H.

The word "Pelican" and the depiction of a pelican are
trademarks of Pelican Publishing Company, Inc., and are
registered in the U.S. Patent and Trademark Office.

Library of Congress Cataloging-in-Publication Data

Harper, Jo, author.
  Whistling Willie from Amarillo, Texas / by Jo and Josephine Harper ; illustrated by
David Harrington.
     pages cm
  Summary: "Young Whistling Willie doesn't look like much of a cowboy. He's smiley and
jolly, not tough and lean. Just the same, he always wanted to be a Texas Ranger. Too bad
they're not interested in having him--until they find out that his powerful whistle can
blow even the meanest ice-cream rustlers into a hole!"-- Provided by publisher.
  ISBN 978-1-4556-2056-2 (hardcover : alk. paper) -- ISBN 978-1-4556-2057-9 (e-book)
[1. Whistling--Fiction. 2. Texas Rangers--Fiction. 3. Amarillo (Tex.)--Fiction. 4. Tall
tales.] I. Harper, Josephine, 1953- author. II. Harrington, David, 1964- illustrator. III.
Title.
  PZ7.H23138Wh 2015
  [E]--dc23

                                              2014044708

Printed in China

Published by Pelican Publishing Company, Inc.
1000 Burmaster Street, Gretna, Louisiana 70053

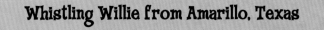

Young **Whistling Willie** didn't look like much of a cowboy even though he always wore a Stetson.

His snakeskin boots and snakeskin belt didn't help. Neither did his fast roan cutting horse and the fact that he never forgot to say "sir" and "ma'am."

Instead of looking tough, he was smiley. And instead of being long and lean, he was pudgy. In fact, his belly was so big you could barely see the silver buckle on his snakeskin belt.

Just the same, Willie wanted to be a **Texas Ranger**. The Rangers were his heroes.

As soon as he was old enough, Whistling Willie tried to join up with the Texas Rangers. On his application, Willie added a note. "I can whistle. I've got a **powerful** whistle."

Willie got a letter back from the Rangers early on the 4th of July. The letter read:

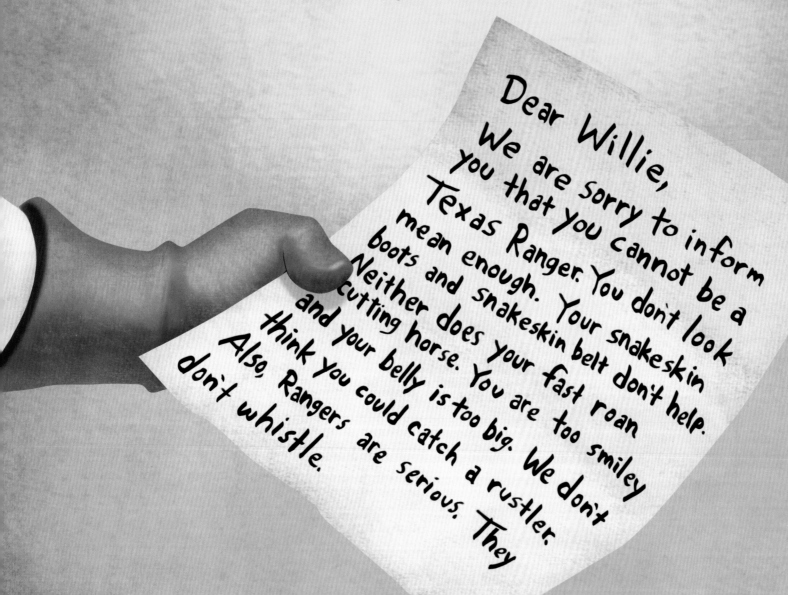

Dear Willie,

We are sorry to inform you that you cannot be a Texas Ranger. You don't look mean enough. Your snakeskin boots and snakeskin belt don't help. Neither does your fast roan cutting horse. You are too smiley and your belly is too big. We don't think you could catch a rustler. Also, Rangers are serious. They don't whistle.

That letter just about broke Willie's heart. He tried hard not to let on, though. He was too kindly to make other folks feel low just because he was downhearted. So he just smiled and whistled softly under his breath.

That afternoon, Willie watched the **4th of July parade** along with everyone else in Amarillo. They all fanned themselves while they admired the high-stepping band, the covered wagons, and the fine cowboys on fox-trotting horses.

It was hot—hot as chili sauce, hot as a dog fight, hot as a branding iron glowing white. But it's supposed to be hot on the 4th of July. Besides, folks knew there was plenty of cold **soda pop** and smooth, cool **ice cream** waiting for them in shady Amarillo Park.

Willie smiled and sweated like everyone else. And he kept on whistling.

But while folks watched the parade, **Sidewinder Slim** and **Corkscrew Slade** rode into town. They were sneaky. They were mean. Those low-down, ornery varmints swilled down all the soda pop and slurped up all the ice cream.

When Mayor Tolliver found out the soda pop and ice cream were gone, he was as mad as a wet hen. Other folks were as mad as hornets. Some were so mad they started spitting nails, and others started pitching hissy fits. But not good-natured Willie. His soft whistle still sounded cheerful. He knew they could always call for the Texas Rangers, so he just took a good long look around.

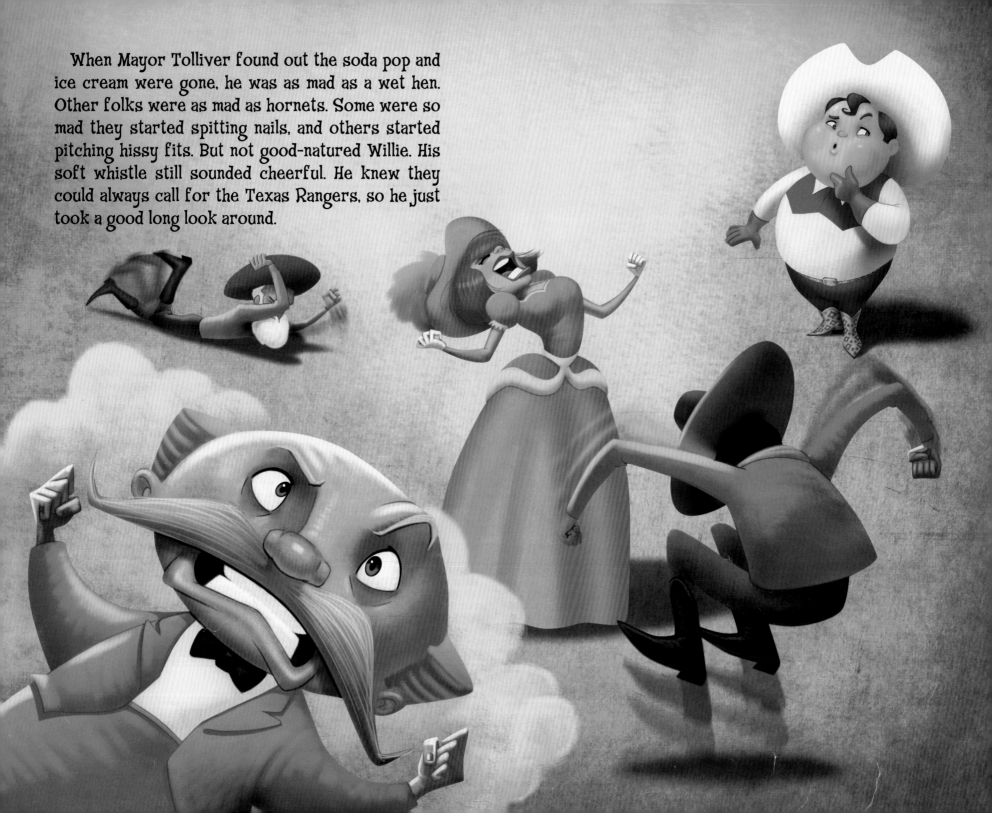

Willie climbed to the top of the water tower and spotted the ice-cream thieves way out on the prairie. He pointed and gave a quick, loud **whistle**.

The high-stepping band, covered wagons, and fine cowboys on fox-trotting horses took off after the scalawags. They chased them through **wheat fields**. They chased them through **corn patches**. They chased them all the way to **Palo Duro Canyon**. But they couldn't catch those slippery varmints.

Back in Amarillo, it was hot as a burning boot. The folks left behind were thirsty and mad enough to bite the head off a hammer—all but Willie.

Mayor Tolliver called the Texas Rangers. "Things are rough in Amarillo," he said. "Send us **Bronco Barker**."

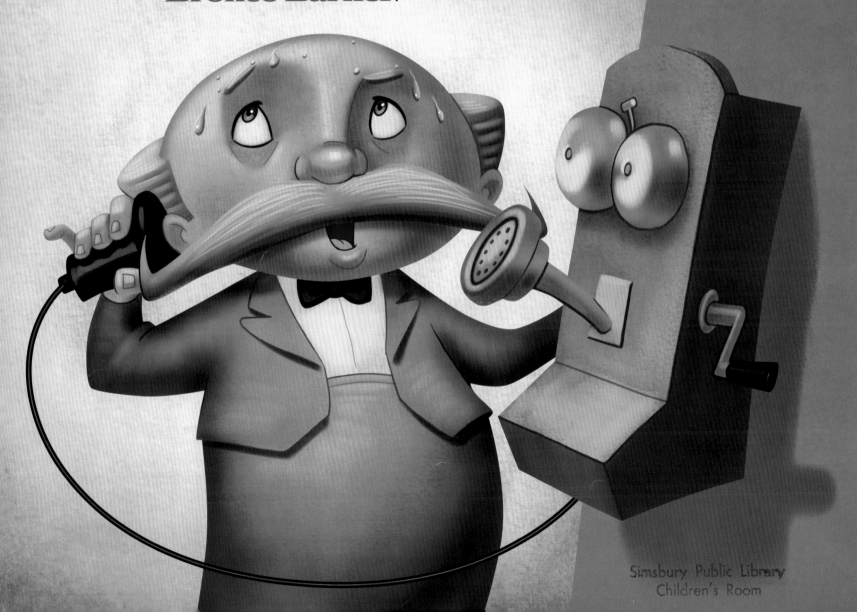

Bronco rode into town like a tornado. He was **long**. He was **lean**. He was **tough**. He was **mean**.

"I cut my teeth on a gun barrel, and I can whip my weight in wolves," he told the crowd. "I'll catch those sneaky scalawags."

But when Bronco looked **high**, Corkscrew Slade and Sidewinder Slim lay **low**. And when he blinked, quick as a hiccup, they were gone.

It was so hot in Amarillo, the fence posts withered.
And folks were on the warpath. Bronco called for
more Rangers to help him.

They galloped into town like a stampede of Brahmas.
Their backs were straight, their bellies were flat, and
their faces were grim, just like Bronco's. Looking at
those Rangers made the folks in Amarillo look grim,
too. All but good-natured Willie. He was still smiling,
and he whistled in admiration of his heroes.

Those Rangers were smart and brave, but the hooligans were slippery-slippery as greased pigs, slippery as oiled eels, slippery as a pocketful of wet worms.

And they **slipped away** from the Rangers.

Willie's heroes were plumb **buffaloed** and **out-coyoted**. They bowed their heads in shame.

That stuck in Willie's craw.

WANTED

CORKSCREW SLADE

SIDEWINDER SLIM

Varmints could slurp up all the ice cream in Amarillo, and it wouldn't ruffle Willie's feathers. They could swill soda pop til the cows came home, and it wouldn't put sand in Willie's gizzard. They could torment the townsfolk from sunup to sundown, and Willie wouldn't get riled. But messing with the Rangers got his goat.

At high noon under the blazing Amarillo sun, Willie
walked to the middle of **Main Street**.

He took a **deep breath** and let out a powerful whistle. He whistled long, and he whistled hard.

As he whistled, a mighty wind, cyclone strong,

and tornado terrible came up from his big belly.

That gale swept through the city of Amarillo and out into the country. It cut through the wheat fields quick as a bullwhip. It sliced through the corn patches plenty pronto. It stormed all the way to Palo Duro Canyon.

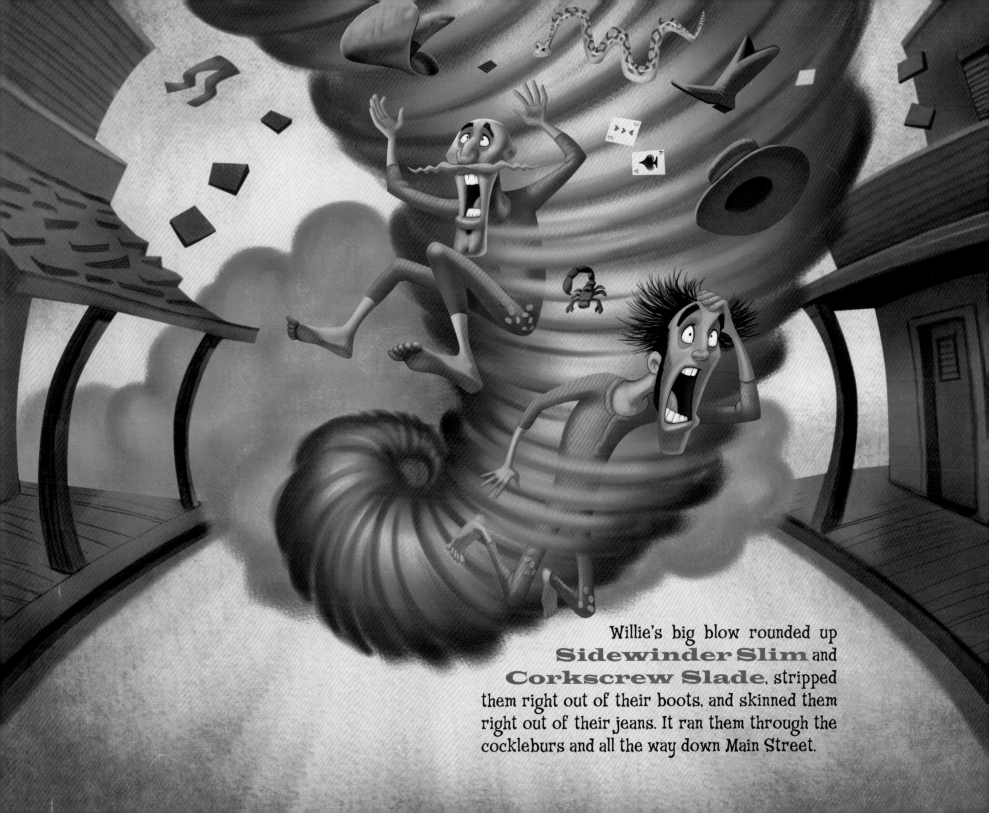

Willie's big blow rounded up
Sidewinder Slim and
Corkscrew Slade, stripped
them right out of their boots, and skinned them
right out of their jeans. It ran them through the
cockleburs and all the way down Main Street.

The folks in Amarillo **laughed** and **slapped their knees**, and those low-down ice-cream rustlers looked for a hole to crawl in. They felt lower than a snake's belly.

The Texas Rangers all smiled at Willie.

One said, "Willie, I like your snakeskin boots and your snakeskin belt." Another said, "I sure admire your fast roan cutting horse." "What I cotton to is your smiley face," said a third.

Bronco Barker pinned a **ranger badge** on Willie. "Pardner, we'd be mighty proud to count you as a Texas Ranger. Do you reckon you could **teach us to whistle?**"

Authors' Note

The Texas Rangers, "men who could not be stampeded," were established with the earliest settlements in Texas. They were unofficially created by Stephen F. Austin in an 1823 call-to-arms. He referred to them as "the Rangers" because they had to range over the entire country. Later, in 1840, Sam Houston commissioned young Jack Coffee Hays to recruit 150 men to Ranger service. Each man had to supply his own horse and gun. Not many men who could afford a horse and gun were willing to work for little more than hardship and danger, so Hays was only able to recruit fifty Rangers. Some Lipan Apaches also joined him as scouts and fighters.

The Rangers came to be a police force, army, and legend. A Texas Ranger was said to "ride like a Mexican, trail like an Indian, shoot like Tennessean, and fight like the devil." Today, there are about 150 Rangers serving throughout the State of Texas. They investigate crimes, round up criminals, and protect the people of the state.

Cox, Mike, "A Brief History of the Texas Rangers," Texas Ranger Hall of Fame and Museum, http://www.texasranger.org/history/BriefHistory1.htm.

Texas Democrat, September 9, 1846, quoted in Walter Prescott Webb, *The Texas Rangers, A Century of Frontier Defense* (Austin: University of Texas, 1935, 1965), 15.

Texas Department of Public Safety, "Historical Development," https://www.txdps.state.tx.us/TexasRangers/HistoricalDevelopment.htm.

Texas Department of Public Safety, "Texas Rangers," https://www.txdps.state.tx.us/TexasRangers/index.htm.